*The Art of Marketing:*
*Innovative Strategies for*
*Entrepreneurs, Startups and*
*eCommerce*

# Table of Contents

# Acknowledgments

*'If you want to go fast, go alone. If you want to go far, go together."* - *Robin Jones Gunn*

Though this is going to be at the beginning the book, I am actually writing this part last as a thank you to everyone who has supported me along the way. Without everyone's help, I would not have had the heart to make what used to be just an idea come to life. The day I posted three variants of my book cover on Facebook -- and receiving one hundred replies in under a day gave me unimaginable hope to finish this book and to put my heart into it. Writing a book can be scary because you are putting yourself out into the world and enabling yourself to be open to criticism, but to be welcomed with open arms is to know one of the best feelings in the world. I am grateful of everything.

The individuals that subscribed to my email list were part of a special group and I counted on them to help me with the launch of my book:

*Thao Nguyen*
*Chris Pham*
*Richard Kieu*
*Andrew Dinh*
*Andy Chiang*
*Christina Nguyen*
*Christian Ancheta*

*Isaac Gomez*
*Star Huynh*
*Edward Vo*
*Bettina Supo*
*Benjamin Nguyen*
*Alfred Ly*
*Esme Orozco*
*Bianca Mellado*
*Tatsuya Ishikawa*
*Kylie Cacao*
*Caren Zeng*
*Jessica Kwong*
*Nancy Chen*
*Cindy Duong*
*Ashari Goins*
*Toral Suthar*
*Manoj Manoj*
*Eric Lee*
*Sarah Belanger*
*Chris Vu*
*Trang Bui*
*Jeremy Cruz*
*Raymond Dang*
*Anthony Dinh*
*Bill Truong*
*Andrew Tani*
*Katie Tran*
*IE Tran*
*Sarah McKee*

Thank you to all who signed up to show me their support. I really do pay individual attention to anyone who supports me and then reaches out to me. It means the world to me.

I'd also like to thank one of my best friends, Jeffrey Nguyen, who was with me every step of the journey from me having the idea for a book to the book turning into a reality. He made me believe that I could write a marketing book at just 19 years old. The time period spent writing this book was filled with many things going on at the same time. There were definitely many low points. It was a struggle to handle everything at once. Working on making this happen meant I had to sacrifice social time to spend more time writing but having him as someone I could talk to whenever I wanted to showed me that though I was alone, I was not lonely. It is not often you can find someone as genuine as him and I am grateful we crossed paths. When I was in my lowest points, he was there to pick me up and support me through difficult times. In my highest points, he will be with me.

I also want to thank the person who made me into the man I am today, Coach Mike. He is a father figure to me and showed me the importance of being a good person. I met him when I was just 11 years old; he was just my soccer coach but despite that, he showed me the path to become the greatest version of myself. He believed in me even before I believed in myself. From a young age, he would always tell me that I was destined to accomplish great things. To be constantly imbued with life lessons and inspiration meant that I had everything I needed to go on and achieve great things. I'm finally just starting to realize what he has been telling me for the past 8 years. From the day he took me in to start weight training to the countless lessons of life all to improve my character, I have constantly been finding who I am as a human being with his support. This is just the start of my journey. Without him, I would never have written this book. Without him, I wouldn't be where I am today. With him, I can move mountains.

*"What happens when an unstoppable force meets an immovable object?"*

Through writing this book, I have learned even more about myself. I have done something I never thought I would've done. I was never one to love writing. In high school, I was a C grade student in English class who dreaded every writing assignment given to me. Who knew I would someday write a book? I had to sacrifice and dedicate more time to writing this book but I recall being told that if you love something, it's not work. I loved writing this book. It tested many of my limits. I'm proud to say that I came out on top. I'm proud to say that together, we came out on top.

# About Me

As you already know, my name is Michael Chen and I am 19 years old. Despite my age, I have never let that stop me from trying to achieve my dreams. Ever since I was young, I had the entrepreneurial spirit. I wanted to learn as much as I could and teach myself many things. I always had the desire to expand my mind. I wanted to be the one to create my own path in life.

When I was 13, I would ask my dad if I could buy wholesale candy from Costco so I can resell it at school to my peers. After school, I would browse the internet and watch exercise videos in order to teach myself how to work out.

When I was 15, I would buy the 32-pack bottled water so I could resell them to people on hot days when there wasn't easy access to drinkable water. Sometimes I even gave full cases of water to the homeless and taught them to resell them, re-invest the money and repeat.

Through my years of high school, I ran Track and Field which pushed me to develop discipline and a hard work ethic. At 17, I ran an online eCommerce business on eBay to sell Apple iPhone cases -- my favorite times were whenever Apple released a new phone. I would also read tons of books to absorb as much knowledge as I can. I even stayed in a classroom at lunch just so I could read. When I was 17, I taught myself photography and had a ton of success holding photo shoots just for friends. Eventually, one set of my photos went viral and I saw success when all my clients came from referrals.

When I was 18, I started my own nonprofit apparel brand, Aspire Higher Apparel. I also taught myself the fundamentals of web design and created my own website (michaelchen.biz).

Now, I am 19 and I've set my courses to write my own marketing book as well as utilize my marketing knowledge as the Marketing Director of Peerbuds (an online personal tutoring startup). Besides that, I've established a subscription box company called Sprightly. It is a blend of nutritional fuel and inspiration for active lifestyles delivered monthly. As you can tell, I am a firm believer that I am the one to decide my destiny. Though I may have supporters, it is ultimately up to me to decide that I want to become the best version of myself. I grew up in the age of the Internet and I fully recognize the power that it has if harnessed correctly. Times really are changing today. It is a new era.

Though I may be young, I never thought I was too young. I have so many things I want to do. Perhaps the biggest thing I want to do is to change this world. I believe even the smallest action can make somebody's world. I want to inspire a generation willing to listen to me and my story. I want this world to be better having me gone through it. This is just the start of my journey.

# Intro

Times are changing in today's digital world. With the boom of new startups and ecommerce platforms, old marketing techniques might not be the best option to draw in potential customers. Marketing techniques and strategies for established corporations are quickly found to be not the best option for new age businesses.

If you are an entrepreneur, founder/part of a startup or in eCommerce, this book is for you.

In *The Art of Marketing: Innovative Strategies for Entrepreneurs, Startups and eCommerce,* I will teach you how to use new and innovative marketing techniques and strategies to build an audience, establish a social media presence using social media and content marketing, improve business/customer relationships and drastically improve your business -- even if you are just starting out.

As the Marketing Director of Peerbuds, founder of a nonprofit apparel brand, blogger, marketing enthusiast and someone who just loves the art of marketing, I have read, utilized and studied hundreds of books and articles on the subject of marketing for the new age of startups and businesses. Whether you are an entrepreneur or college dropout who decided to start a business or both, you will benefit from this book by implementing the how-tos, tips and tricks used by many of the greatest startups and businesses you know today.

Companies like Airbnb, Dropbox, Uber, Instagram and literally thousands more have all used and benefitted from strategies that are found in this exact book -- and you can too.

I promise that if you use what you learn from *The Art of Marketing: Innovative Strategies for Entrepreneurs, Startups and eCommerce,* you will see an increase in users, improve the image of your business, draw more attention from potential customers, help them solve their needs and ultimately lead them to purchase your product or service.

Many marketing books all have one mistake in common: they are intended to be learned in classroom environments. They are too theoretical and difficult to utilize in a practical situation. However, this book will teach you actionable strategies you will be able to use the very same day.

Don't be the person who misses out on the incredible opportunity to learn and use these effective marketing techniques today. Be the kind of person others look at and say "I don't know how they did it. I wish I knew what they knew". Be the kind of person who takes action today.

The things you are about to learn will catapult your success in business by using effective and proven marketing strategies that modern companies today are using. Each chapter will teach you something new and something you can use today. Pick up your copy of *The Art of Marketing: Innovative Strategies for Entrepreneurs, Startups and eCommerce!*

# What Is Marketing?

The best product in the world means nothing if no one knows about it.

The purpose of marketing is to attract attention to your product or to create interest which will ultimately lead to a profit. The best thing is that there are so many ways to achieve that. The worst thing is that there are *so* many ways to achieve that. It is a double-edged sword. There are so many ideas that it will seem overwhelming to know what to use, how to use it and when to use it. Fortunately, I have compiled the best tactics for you in this book.

Marketing focuses on having new ideas, thinking smarter, executing and exuding creativity with passion.

I am inspired by social media expert and entrepreneur, Gary Vaynerchuk's idea that cash is oxygen. Without cash to run your business, you will go out of business. It doesn't matter if you have the best idea, best plan or the best team. If you have no cash, you have a very limited time to find a way to get more cash or you will go out of business. I want to prevent that.

I believe that the best marketing is based on genuinely helping people solve their problem. It cannot be focused on sales or pushing your product to  a potential customer's face if they don't want it. It is ultimately about making a better world. Honesty is one of the best investments. You should have complete confidence in the product you are selling so it will benefit both you and them.

# Startup vs. Corporation

Startup marketers need to differentiate themselves from traditional marketers for established corporations that have been here for many decades. They need to have a different set of tools and a knack for innovation. This has led to a new way of marketing called growth hacking.

Here are three reasons why startups need to market differently:

**Startups intend to grow exponentially over a short period of time**
The goal of many startups is to go from zero to millions of users in a few short years. Starting from the beginning, startups need to grow very fast because they do not have an established customer base as opposed to seasoned corporations that aim to keep steady the growth they have already acquired.

**Startups have a blank slate**
Since they don't have an established customer base yet, startups can afford to use new ways to extend their reach out into the world. They can afford to break the rules, think creatively and test out innovative ways that might work or not. Established corporations already have an image and they will have a very difficult time overcoming old perceptions.

**Startups do not have the same amount of resources and funding**

This calls for an increased need for innovation--find new ways to do more with less. Growth hacking. They simply do not have enough resources as compared to corporations that may have a dedicated marketing budget. If startups fail to figure out how to market quickly enough the right way, they will go out of business.

Fortunately, I have laid out all the tools for you in the upcoming chapters so you can take advantage of the growth hack techniques and strategies that startups have been using to launch their brand off the ground.

# Growth Hacking

As mentioned earlier, using growth hacking strategies is the best way to grow your brand. What is growth marketing though? To find out more about it, we'll go back to its origins when the term "growth hacker" was coined by Sean Ellis.

Sean Ellis was the person everyone went to when they needed ideas on how to grow their startups. He created systems, strategies and mindsets that were different from traditional marketing. Over time, he has helped many startups increase their brand exposure, user base and profit. Now, Sean had to eventually train others to replace him in the future but whenever he received a resume, it would be a resume suited for a traditional marketing position. He didn't want traditional marketers to take his place. Sure, they were great resumes, but they weren't suited for the position that was to be replaced.

Early in a startup, you don't need someone to build and manage a marketing team. You don't have the budget to have a dedicated marketing team. You don't need a plan to sustain the users you already have. You don't have enough users yet.

Early in a startup, you *need* growth.

Sean quotes that "a growth hacker is a person whose true north is growth". By truly focusing on any system, strategy, or tactic dedicated on driving growth, they are able to exponentially grow a startup fast.

Now, instead of asking for marketers, Sean asks for growth hackers.

With the increased presence of the Internet in the world, the word *product* is quickly being redefined. Having a tangible product is still grounds for being called a product. But what about internet products? Software? Apps? Platforms like Facebook, Dropbox, Instagram are all internet-only products. Growth hackers simply need to have a different set of tools.

Growth hackers are trying to find ways on how they can build a self-sustaining marketing machine into their products. The product itself is the vehicle. With the Internet, there are plenty of tools that allow growth hackers to take the guessing out of their strategies. Nowadays, growth hackers are able to track, test and question whether the method they are using is viable. Taking a guess if their strategy was working is not on a growth hacker's agenda.

A great example of a startup integrating their own self-sustaining marketing machine is Buffer. Buffer is a software that allows users to schedule and upload posts automatically to Twitter and Facebook. It solved a need that allowed people to focus less on being reminded that it is time to post so they can focus on other things. You can post in your sleep. With Buffer's free feature, every post is tagged with the Buffer symbol. With more and more people using Buffer, they automatically get more exposure. More people using Buffer will bring more users to Buffer because they are spreading it with the post tag. The system runs itself. With an integrated system to analyze clicks and views, users don't have to guess whether or not their posts are getting attention. They are also able to view which kind of posts gather the most attention and so they can post more of what works. This is growth hacking.

You can see how different this way of marketing would be from traditional marketing. Big corporations would usually buy advertising space in Times Square or spend millions of dollars on having a spot in something popular like the Macy's Thanksgiving Parades. It is great for exposure, but they aren't able to track how many people see their ad and how many were compelled to buy their product. They can only hope it worked.

This isn't to say that traditional marketing is worse than growth hacking. Traditional marketing has a wider set of tools that can cast a wider net. Both sides are equally powerful in helping the corporation or startup in achieving their goals. The main focus here is to use the one that best  helps you achieve your goals. Growth hackers are just forced to be innovative with ways to cultivate growth. They don't have the resources. On a side note, growth hacking is not just limited to startups. Corporations can also utilize growth hacks. Imagine what can happen if they combine growth hacking with resources...

Ryan Holiday was the director of marketing at American Apparel, a company that focused heavily on traditional marketing. However, he quickly learned the term "growth hacker" and has come to understand the power of it. He has even written a book called *Growth Hacker Marketing*. In his book, he comes to understand that:

*"A growth hacker is someone who has thrown out the playbook of traditional marketing and replaced it with only what is testable, trackable, and scalable. Their tools are emails, pay-per-click ads, blogs and platform APIs instead of commercials, publicity, and money. [...] growth hackers relentlessly pursue users and growth -- and when they do it right, those users beget more users, which beget more users. They are the inventors [...] of their own self-sustaining and self propagating growth machine that can take a startup from nothing to something."*

## Best of Both Worlds

A growth hacker must combine creativity and analytics together if they are to succeed. One is not better than the other. Growth hackers are urged to be innovative, think of new crazy ideas that may or may not work and be courageous enough to do something never seen before. Take for example, Airbnb, the startup that allows people to turn their home or apartment into a spot that people can rent for a certain period of time. At the beginning stages, people at Airbnb needed to find a way to acquire more users and drive their exposure. They came up with a genius way. They decided they will piggyback off of Craigslist's popularity. The problem was that Craigslist did not have a public API that easily made it for others to integrate their services into it. That wasn't going to stop the Airbnb growth hackers. They reverse engineered their way into Craigslist and successfully set up a bridge between their platform and Craigslist. For a time, users were given an option to cross-post their Airbnb listing to Craigslist, exponentially increasing their exposure. Eventually, Craigslist put an end to this but if Airbnb never took the chance to try this crazy experiment, who knows where they would be today. They saw a chance and they took it. They innovated.

Now that we've talked about the importance of creativity in growth hacking, we will move onto another important aspect: analytics.

Analytics are extremely important because it grants growth hackers vision. Using analytics, they are able to see what works and what doesn't. This is called A/B testing. It is exactly what it sounds like! Is "A" working or is "B" working? Whatever is working, they will focus, repeat and see if it works another time around. Using analytical tools such as KISSmetrics, they are able to track their success -- or lack of it. If a startup finds that they are getting 40% of all their users from conversions in their email list, they will focus more on that in order to keep driving growth. Without analytics, a growth hacker will be operating blindly.

All these words about analytics, A/B testing and numbers make it sound like to be a growth hacker, you need to know how to code or be a programmer. I don't believe this is true. Although there is coding or programming involved in growth hacking, there are different roles that a person can take. For example, there could be three people on a team. A front end developer (makes it presentable), a backend developer (codes and programs) and the idea machine. The idea machine can come up with ideas, discuss it with the back end developer to see if it is possible to create and the front end developer will be able to push it out to the public. There are also possibilities that a person can be all three. This person is very valuable to any startup. You can even ditch coding altogether and find the best growth hack suited for your own business. For example, if you are marketing your own eCommerce business, you can use Instagram and use strategies like showcasing Influencers, getting guest blog posts or holding contests. I'll elaborate further about it  in the Instagram Marketing Chapter. However, this goes to show that you do not need to know how to code or program to be a growth hacker.

**Strategies you can expect from this book**

As we learned before, growth hackers do not have a huge dedicated budget for marketing. The best way to get more exposure, users and business is to find ways to pull them in without breaking the bank. Fortunately, this book is full of "pull" methods to help you achieve your goals. With these "pull" strategies, you don't have to go out and "push" them toward your product or service. You draw them in with *valuable* content that will solve their need, which will inevitably help improve your business. Keyword: valuable. Providing value to your users will keep them by your side. One example of "pull" strategies is content marketing which includes blogs, SEO, infographics, etc. An example of a "push" strategy is paid advertising. While "pull" strategies are the most cost-effective, I have also included certain "push" strategies that will also help you. If you do have some to spend on this type of marketing, you can reap the rewards. Remember, one is not better than the other. It is a matter of finding what works for your particular situation. If you can combine both, then you are well equipped to lift your business off the ground!

# Common Mistakes In Marketing

*"Learn from the mistakes of others. You cannot live long enough to make them all yourself."* -Groucho Marx

Before we can learn what to do in marketing, it is important to learn *what we shouldn't do* so we can avoid them altogether by being aware of them. After all, learning from others' mistakes can teach us just as well as making them ourselves.

**Bad quality content**

Content that solves a person's need is content a person wants to read.

Whether it may be something funny to look at, something informative or something educational, a person will look at it if it interests, provides value or is relevant to them.

Your task is to figure out what your target market wants and then give it it to them. Are you a blogger focused on self-help articles? Many people in the self improvement niche love to read motivational success stories because it gives them something tangible to believe that they can do it too.

On platforms like Instagram, visuals play the most important role. If you can put out quality content that is visually appealing, people will follow you to see what you will upload next. Find out what is interesting to your target market and use it to your advantage.

## Running out of steam

Many times, a business will start off very strong and push out all of their content all at once.

Everything is going great but then they quickly find out that they are running out of ideas. They aren't sure of their next move.

To avoid this, using a marketing plan and organizing your moves (which I will teach you later in this book) will allow you to decide what to do each step of the way in order to keep your momentum rolling.

Don't run out of steam. Let the world know "I still exist!"

## Failing to build anticipation

People want what they can't have -- yet.

A ton of entrepreneurs have *supplied* great products. But where is the *demand*?

Don't forget that one of the most important points to make  your product or service do well is to create demand before the product is released.

I have seen many cases in which there is definitely a great product but no one knows about it.

Then the product creators must build a customer base while the product is already out which ruins the anticipation and decreases the number of conversions in contrast to building up demand before launching the product.

**Importance of Mobile**

Nowadays, the majority of people have a smartphone.

This means they can be connected to the world by pulling out a device from their pockets. In 2014, the number of mobile users surpassed the number of desktop users. The number is only going to rise in 2016. This is because of the fast paced "I want it now" environment that many of us now live in.

On your phone, you can

- "Walk" Times Square
- Pay your bills
- Press the right buttons for pizza at your doorstep
- Say hello to mom and dad 300 miles away
- Explore the world on your toilet

Your goal is to optimize your mobile presence. Many people focus on their website but forget to configure it for mobile use. People forget that many users land on their website while browsing on their phone. Get your business to their phone through a mobile friendly website, create mobile apps or establish a presence on mobile social media apps.

Now that we've gone over some of the most common mistakes made in marketing, we can combat them by learning from others' mistake and doing it the right way. Don't worry. Later on in this book, you will learn the strategies that will keep you from making these mistakes and paying dearly for them.

# Through The Looking Glass

How do you reply when someone asks what your company does?

By having a crystal clear brand message, you should be able to summarize your company's message in one sentence.

Every company needs a voice. Your brand message helps communicate to the world what your ideals and values are.

In the best case scenario, your brand message will help strengthen your brand, your mission and the reason that makes people purchase your product instead of other brands. On the other hand, poor brand messaging will confuse your market and can make you lose a large number of people who otherwise would have been your customers.

Brand messages can take all sorts of forms -- taglines, slogans, elevator pitches, etc.

They all share a common trait in which they are all concise and clarify the most important part of your brand.

Here are some examples of great brand messages. I'm sure you've heard of them.

- Walmart: Save Money. Live Better.

- Burger King: Have It Your Way.

- IMAX: Think Big.

- Nike: Just Do It.

- Disneyland: The Happiest Place on Earth.

*How do I create a crystal clear brand message?*

**Decide on the writing style**
1. Start with the tone, choice of vocabulary and style. There are brands that have a humorous style (eHarmony) and there are brands that want to convey power and craftsmanship (Aston Martin).

**Create an elevator pitch**
2. The elevator pitch will allow you to tell people who your brand is, what you do and why they should buy your product or service in 30 seconds. This is very effective in introducing your brand to a large number of people. It also makes it easy for them to remember what your brand is about.

**Create your positioning statement**
3. The positioning statement is one sentence that will summarize your brand's values. This is a great place to differentiate yourself from other brands. What makes you unique?

**Create your mission statement**
4. What are you here for? What is your "why?" Apple wanted to revolutionize technology. Facebook wanted to connect the world. Your mission statement should also be concise (one sentence).

**Create a slogan or tagline**
5. Like the brands we just went over, your slogan should also be catchy and memorable for your market. It should be concise and specific. It can be one word or a few words. Your slogan is widely used in your advertisements and campaigns so be sure to get creative.

*Can I ever change these?*

Keep in mind that while you should keep every one of these components consistent, you can change them later in the future.

This is the process called *rebranding.*

Be careful though as rebranding can result in a disaster if you change only one component that strays too far from your core ideals.

Successful rebranding involves changing your mission, goals and visions. Basically, they should all be consistent at all times.

*What do I use all of these for?*

Everything you communicate to your market. Your advertisements, website, campaigns, events, sales copy etc. Your brand message is your overarching theme. Show it to the world.

# Power of the People

There is no doubt about it. People are the driving force behind every single part of your business. If no one purchased your product or came to you for business, you will go out of business. Utilizing the power of the people can astronomically improve your business.

By being a business for the people, you will be more profitable, you cultivate brand loyalty and you become more respectable in the eyes of the world.

Don't forget that because they are human beings, all of your actions should always be backed with ethics, moral and respect. You should never abuse your power. You wouldn't want to be a disservice to anyone and waste anyone's time.

There are a certain number of strategies to win over their hearts. I have used and studied the most effective ways that entrepreneurs, startups and eCommerce businesses are using to take their business off the ground.

### Influencers

How many times do you see people wearing the newest clothes because they are trending or in style?

The reason why those clothes are in style is because they've seen the biggest stars wearing them and so they go out and buy the same clothes. They've seen the most popular magazines showcasing them and so they believe that is the new thing to wear.

People tend to follow other people especially when those people have major influence in that niche.

Now, this doesn't apply to just clothes. You can virtually make anything "cool" by connecting with people that are popular in that niche.

I don't mean if you want to promote your clothes, you have to get Kanye West to wear them.

Utilizing bloggers, journalists, famous Instagrammers, YouTubers or just anyone who has a presence and who has the same message as you will drive your brand awareness to new heights.

**IMPORTANT:** You shouldn't just go after any influencer. It matters that you go after the RIGHT influencers: the one that fits your product and market.

You can start small and slowly build up a respectable reputation in order to eventually reach the big leagues.

Here are two of the most effective ways to connecting with Influencers:

## 1. Introduce yourself

- Send over a quick email complimenting them on their work. Show them praise but don't be a kiss-up.

- Share their work on your media outlets.

- Leave a heartfelt comment on their posts.

- Write a positive review for their product

- Do what you can to get on their radar BUT...

- **DO NOT** annoy or spam them. Use your social awareness.

- **DO NOT** directly ask for a shoutout or mention. This can be seen as rude and end your relationship before it even starts.

## 2. Give

*"Give, give, give and you shall receive."*

I am about to tell you one of the most important things to keep in mind when you are interacting with people. Do not abuse it.

The Rule of Reciprocation states that "we should try to repay, in kind, what another person has provided us." - Robert B. Cialdini, Ph.D, author of *Influence: The Psychology of Persuasion.*

This applies to all your interactions with everyone. Whether you are networking or building a relationship as business partners or making a new friend, make yourself valuable by providing something to them. It doesn't have to be a physical object or a gift. It will be something in return you give to them as a reminder that you value them and their time.

**IMPORTANT:**
Remember to always give without expecting **anything** in return. Being genuine in your actions will take you further than if you give with an ulterior motive.

It is up to them if they decide to return your gesture.

So what can you do? Just keep giving and eventually you will receive even when you don't expect anything in return.

**Word of Mouth**

Word of mouth has been considered one of the most powerful tools in marketing. People are more prone to believe people they know. If you heard your best friend talking about how well this product worked or a large number of people giving great reviews, you would be very interested to see what it can do for you right? Successful word of mouth marketing will lead to many positive reviews, testimonials and referrals which will lead to more sales.

There are 3 components of successful word of mouth marketing. They are called the 3 E's.

1.      Engage: Interact with the people. Be active in the community. This can be done by responding actively to people's comments, questions, concerns or by posing questions to drive engagement in the community.

2.      Equip: Give the people something to talk about. Do something remarkable that will have them talking about you.

3.      Empower: Present a chance for your community to feel special. This can be done by holding polls on which design of t-shirt should be released next. Conduct customer feedback campaigns. Give the people a voice and opinion.

One of my favorite examples of word of mouth marketing comes from The Dollar Shave Club. I've seen them reply *consistently* to user comments on Facebook and Instagram-- and in return, I've seen people give them praise for being so active in their community. They've also partnered with another company to provide free razors to the United States Military. This caused people that otherwise wouldn't have been their customers to purchase their product. I've seen many comments posted about people telling their friends about the company and that they will spread the word. If that doesn't sound like successful word of mouth marketing, I don't know what is.

**Brand Ambassadors**
Another way to take advantage of word of mouth marketing is to create a Brand Ambassador program.

Brand Ambassadors are essentially people who are passionate about your brand and who want to promote it. They are real people and they enjoy representing your brand. They talk about your brand regularly and get compensated in return -- either monetarily or free clothing items, commission, exclusive access, etc. Having a real person represent your brand positively and spread it to their friends, family and network will surely increase your brand awareness. Do you want greater positive exposure leading to profitability? Your brand ambassadors are the key to that.

The secret to creating a successful brand ambassador program is to create a win-win situation for both parties.

An example of a great brand ambassador program was the Google Pizza Program. This program's goal was for the ambassador to walk around elite engineering university cafeterias and buy them a pizza -- on Google's behalf. Included in this program were free shirts and items and it became a successful program. It created a win-win situation for the ambassador. They got free Google Swag and for the engineering students who received a free pizza… well they got to eat for the day considering how expensive university tuition is. Google's image was promoted to top engineering students, the type of people they want to work at their company.

Be creative.

Even if your brand doesn't have too much to offer just yet, find a way to compensate them by either combining monetary rewards from commission, free swag, shoutouts, and access to exclusive early releases. There are so many more ways once you discover what you can give. Your brand ambassadors are part of your team. Treat them well.

**Storytelling**

Remember when you were young and your parents would read you a bedtime story before you went to sleep and you had dreams of that story? Stories are more prone to stick in your head -- and you would want to have your market think about you as the first thing that comes to mind.

People are attracted to relatable content. People are attracted to stories.

Since the age of the cavemen, humans have been communicating with stories. Stories have the power to invoke emotions, give reasons, build trust and ultimately connect people.

A great example of storytelling was expertly done by the company Teleflora. Teleflora delivers flowers and they take advantage of every Valentine's Day to ramp up their marketing. In a short ad, titled *What Is Love?,* Teleflora was able to capture the powerful emotions of love. They dug deep into our emotions with beautiful imagery, compelling music, the happiness of love and the pain of heartbreak. The ad was very effective because it hit all the points that a person can relate too. In turn, many people immediately reached out to their loved ones and used Teleflora's service. It was a success.

In the content that you create, try to tell a story that will capture your market's attention and appeal to their emotions.

# Generating Anticipation

Generating anticipation around your product is very important. Many call this "creating buzz". Either way, creating a demand for your product before it even comes out can be a great way to get validation and catapult your launch to be more successful than ever before.

An important thing to remember is that creating buzz takes time. With strategic timing, making your market excited about the release of your product will be easier than ever before. Over a few months, ideally a product can build enough anticipation to go viral once it is released.

People want what they can't have.

In their early days, Dropbox was not open to the public. People had to sign up to a list and wait to join. Later, they combined this with creating a fun and engaging video about how to use their product that went viral. Immediately, Dropbox saw an exponential increase in the number of people who were itching to sign up to the waiting list hoping the day to finally use Dropbox would come sooner.

Apple is notorious for creating an illusion of scarcity. With the release of the new iPhone 6, they sold 10 million units on the day of launch. They reported on their website that due to high demand, deliveries will be delayed. They do this because it makes people perceive their phones as being in demand and more desirable. Nothing draws a crowd like a crowd. People had to wait to get their hands on the new product which fueled even more demand.

Here are a couple of ways you can create anticipation:

1.     Make a limited time offer to encourage your market to take action as quick as they can

2.     Utilize a pre-release to create a feeling of exclusivity. The most effective people to give early access to your product are Influencers. "That person over there has that great product, how can I get it too?" Facebook knew this and launched only for Harvard students in their early days. Look at them now.

3.     Encourage people to sign up to a waiting list to get early access to your product. This is a great time to communicate with the people who sign up to your waiting list to provide more insider info and fuel more demand.

4.     Make your product invite only **OR** Make a referral program in which a person has to bring a friend or two in order to sign up. This will give you two to three times the exposure and create a community surrounding your product.

5.     Take pre-orders. Even if you're not a new company and already have a product on the line, your

existing customers who love the product you've already put out will be eager to get their hands on your new releases.

6.    Create mystery. While you may not be as big as Apple, you can still create mystery by hinting your product and how it will help people solve their problems. Give sneak peeks of your product without giving too much away. The key? Be mysterious but let people know that something great that can solve their problems are coming.

# Content Marketing

Content marketing is all about putting the right content in the right place at the right time. It is about creating free content that will educate people and provide them with value that will attract them to your whole business. It is not centered on selling, rather making everyone who consumes your content become more intelligent or get entertained. By constantly providing valuable insight to visitors, we build trust and they will be more inclined to reward us with their business or share us to spread the word.

Take a look at many of the product pitches you see everywhere from businesses trying to directly sell their product to you. Can you say spammy? All they do is talk about their product trying to get you to buy it. It rarely provides any real information other than a couple of FAQs . Then, their pamphlet or pitch to you ends up in the trash. This is why content marketing, when done correctly, is so effective. It makes readers want to stop what they are doing. They read, look and learn.

One of my favorite examples of successful content marketing is by GoPro. GoPro is a company that creates small cameras that can be attached to a person to enable hands-free use. Their cameras are used all around the world for action shots, extreme sports and even for the average user going on vacation in Hawaii. The nature of GoPro attracts people that are into adventures, exploration action sports and most important of all, visuals. GoPro knows this and they are making great decisions by uploading quality and visually appealing videos that inspire people to get up out of their seats and go skydiving (that may be a little extreme). They also love to upload stunning photos. The point is... it works. GoPro has over 8 million Instagram followers who are highly engaged with liking, posting comments and tagging their friends so they can also view beautiful imagery. They focus on what people would want and they sure can deliver.

There are many content marketing tools but we will focus on social media and blogging. I believe these two are the most powerful tools to gain traction for businesses as they combine to create valuable content that people all around the world will see. With blogging and social media, there are many underlying strategies you can utilize. I will teach you how to use them so you can get started on improving your business!

Let's start with social media.

**Social Media**

What if I told you that there is a free and effective way your business can reach millions of people?

I am about to tell you one of the most important aspects of marketing that will bring you dividends of growth and exposure that will exponentially skyrocket your business off the ground.

Are you ready?

It is tapping into the power of social media.

In today's digital age, if you are not taking advantage of social media, you are losing out. It is as simple as that.

Here are some of the most important statistics that was found by the marketing experts over at HubSpot, Social Media Examiner and eMarketer.

1. **27% of total US internet time** is spent on social networking sites.

2. **92 % of all marketers** indicate that investing in social media results in more exposure for their businesses.

3. **33 % of consumers** discover new brands, products and services on social networks.
4. **Approximately 46% of online users** rely on social media when they make a buying decision.

What does this mean? It means you should get social. Now.

Social media is a vital component of marketing in the digital age. It is a free, effective and efficient way of getting your brand out into the world. Why is this important if you are an entrepreneur, part of a startup or running an eCommerce business? The answer is that the nature of our field is that we have a limited marketing budget. We can't go out and purchase billboard space in Times Square or even on the side of the freeway. Social media solves this problem.

As I mentioned earlier in this book, many people have access to a smartphone that allows them to be capable of accessing apps like Facebook, Instagram, Twitter, Snapchat, Google+ and LinkedIn all at the touch of a button (or screen). Instantly, they can stumble upon your business, startup or online store just by looking through their phone.

You might not be as big as Coca-Cola and there might not be as much people out there who  trust you. Social media is a great way to bring in potential customers and show them that you are an established business, that you know your stuff and that you are the real deal. Building relationships with your market is one of the most important things you need to do and social media will allow you to leverage that aspect.

The internet has changed the speed of which people communicate with others. For example, someone can comment on your Facebook that they have some questions before they buy your product and you will be able to respond as quickly as you can before they lose interest. That resulted to  another customer. Another person finds your Instagram page and loves the photos that you upload. It appeals to her  and now she is  interested in finding out more about your product. Then she  tags her  friends and comments " @bestfriendxo thought you might find this interesting!" They both buy your product and suddenly you have two more customers who you wouldn't have had if you weren't on social media.

Now, you can't take advantage of using social media that easily. Maintaining your social media channels takes work and commitment. You **MUST** upload great content that makes people want to spread it out to their network. Aside from uploading great content, you must be consistent with your schedule of posts. Apps like Buffer can help you in scheduling posts for Facebook and Twitter that automatically gets uploaded at a time you've set. If you can capture what people care about and what inspires them, you will be successful in getting the attention of the internet. The more quality content you share that entertains or solves people's problems, the more traffic that comes to you.

The key to being successful on social media lies in having the right strategy suited to your business and the market you are trying to reach.

Here are things you should consider when creating your social media marketing strategy:

> **1. Choose your voice** on social media. This goes back to what we talked about the Through the Looking Glass chapter. Are you going to be more serious or more laid back?

**2. Define your goals.** As entrepreneurs or startups, we should leverage the power of social media to:

- **Build brand awareness.** As you strategically post, engage and interact with your market, you will naturally get your name out there.

- **Show your goods.** Post content about your product and services to show people what you can bring to the table. What can you do that will solve their problems? Having quality content people care about will make them want to share your content which furthers your exposure. Other people advertising for you? That is something you want. That is something we all want. That is something you can achieve.

- **Build trust.** As I mentioned earlier, building a relationship with users is crucial to your business. As a new business that doesn't have the following of an established corporation, you need to build trust with users. Interacting personally with people will put a humanly aspect to your business. Don't be faceless.

- **Get more business.** After raising brand awareness, solving people's problem, building a relationship and ultimately acquiring a new customer, congratulations! If you've successfully used social media as a way to get more customers, you've used social media right.

**3. Choose your social media platform.** Use the platform that your target market uses. Be sure not to spread yourself out too thin. Start with one to three platforms and focus on those. Remember, quality over quantity.

- **Facebook.** The jack of all trades. If you are not sure where to start, Facebook will be the best option to reach a great number of people. Share blog posts, photos, advertise using dark posts (I'll explain this soon) and interact with users all in one place. All credible businesses have a Facebook. You should too.

- **Instagram.** My personal favorite. Users can only share photos and because of this, Instagram is a HIGHLY visual platform. Using beautiful visuals to entertain, engage, and spread your content is one of the most effective ways to build a profitable business. I will go more in depth of how to tap into the benefits of Instagram later. Instagram is so important that it gets its own section!

- **Twitter.** This is a great platform for more personalized interaction with users. It is also a great place for content distribution. It's perfect for bloggers as Twitter is link-friendly.

- **YouTube.** Can you create high quality videos that can capture a lot of attention? YouTube is great way to build brand awareness. People love high-quality and visually stimulating content. Say your startup offers fitness products or services. You can upload 3-minute videos that teach viewers how to do a squat or deadlift. These are great ways for viewers to convert into customers.

- **LinkedIn.** The more professional Facebook. It is great for global and business-to-business (B2B) networking.

Here are some helpful strategies you can use on social media today:

**Facebook Dark Posts (Advertising)**

Renowned multimillionaire entrepreneur Gary Vaynerchuk stresses the power of Facebook Dark Posts. Now, at first, it sounds like dark posts are evil. It has nothing to with that. If anything, they are good! Imagine if you could get your advertisement right smack dab in the center Facebook Newsfeeds of your ideal audience. Serve the hungry a plate of food because that is what dark posts are. Dark posts are highly customizable advertisements in which you can choose your target audience (demographics, age, interests etc.) and Facebook will automatically send your advertisement to their newsfeeds as they are scrolling down. You are literally reaching the exact people you need to reach.

I constantly see Dollar Shave Club's advertisements on my newsfeed because they are smart. I am part of their target audience because they sell quality razors to shave facial hair. I am a 19 year old male that potentially has facial hair I need to shave off. Sadly, I don't have enough facial hair to shave daily and invest my money in them but you get the point.

Dark posts are called this because you can post without posting to your Facebook page and disrupting your already established audience. It is perfect for A/B testing to find out which type of advertising works because you can run multiple variations of your ads to review the best performance. No, these advertisements aren't on the right side of the screen like you normally see but right down the middle where they are looking. Depending on how specific or broad you choose for your audience, you can reach millions of people -- people that can actually be interested in your product. While I do prefer not to spend money on advertising and instead use inbound marketing strategies, I do understand the advantage of using Facebook Dark Posts. You can even set it up to allow a daily budget or a lifetime budget so you have no risk of overspending on your budget. You can choose to spend $1 a day or even $1000 as a lifetime budget. It's all up to you. To set up a dark post, find the Facebook Ad Manager and Facebook will guide you from there.

Using eye catching visuals will help you get even more attention. Be sure to use catchy headlines and descriptions to get your target audience to convert. Set your ad to run when your audience is most engaged, like during prime time. Know your audience and give them what they want.

**Hold a competition, contest or giveaway.**

I personally have had a lot of success holding a giveaway. People love free stuff! You can give away something physical or digital. When I held a giveaway for my nonprofit apparel brand, I saw user engagement go up exponentially. You can ask for users to follow, like or share your page in return for a chance to win your product for free. For a repost contest, you can utilize a unique hashtag you made up on Instagram and ask users to post an image with your product with the hashtag in order to win something for free. If you're low on funding and can't afford to give away a product for free, I find that creating something digital that has unlimited distribution value is a great alternative. By a digital product, I mean something as simple as a personalized thank you email, a mention on your page or an information product that will teach them something. A great example of a company using these methods is Frank Body. Frank Body sells coffee grind exfoliation products for healthy skin. They are experts in utilizing user engagement to spread their brand name. Their Instagram page is curated focused -- meaning they select lucky users that post an image with their product to be featured on their page with a multimillion follower base. What a great incentive to repost their product! Frank Body gets free exposure around the world and users lucky enough to be chosen for a feature are seen by millions of other users. Talk about instant fame!

**Know the current trends.**

Is it Super Bowl season? Is it close to Christmas? Halloween? Is there something big going on that many people are interested at the moment? Take advantage of trends to create content that relate to them. One of my favorite examples is how Starbucks runs a Christmas/Holiday themed cup promotion. People wait all year round to order their favorite holiday themed drink. Here's another great example. During the moments leading up to the release of the movie *Deadpool*, Tinder, one of the fastest growing speed dating apps, agreed to a promotional opportunity in which the character Deadpool could be seen as you swipe left through the sea of speed-daters. Swipe right on Deadpool to learn more information about the movie. Genius.

**Actively interact with people**

Some brands make the mistake of using their social media to only promote their products or services. This is not the way to go as it is should be about the customer and you -- not you all the time. Cultivate trust by putting a face to your brand. Let people know you're not a faceless corporation and that you genuinely care about them. When someone asks a question, respond as quickly as you can. When someone shows appreciation for how your product helped them, respond with genuine gratitude. Spark conversations with people. Build a community around your brand. Giving the people a voice in your company makes them feel really special. A way to achieve this is to hold a survey asking for feedback about how you can improve as a brand to help better solve their problems. As mentioned earlier, the people over at Dollar Shave Club are doing an excellent job of engaging with their audience. In turn, they make profit from excellent user interaction. I promise you that if you show that you genuinely care about the people, it will come back to you.

**Be aware of your image**

Always keep in mind the voice of your brand. Are you being consistent using it? In terms of social media platforms that show "followers" and who you follow, be sure to always try to keep the number of "followers" more than the number of "following". Having a higher "following" count than "followers" makes your brand come off as spammy and unprofessional. Don't spam your content all at once on a given day. Be careful of unsolicited messaging -- it can be annoying and come off as spam. Double check the quality of content you are posting. Always keep it high quality so people can take you seriously.

**Look at what your competitors are doing**

This does not mean copying exactly what they are doing. Analyze what they are doing right and find out how you can implement that into your own brand by putting a spin on it. On the flip side, see what they are doing wrong and find out how you can leverage what they are missing. Remember what I said about learning from other people's mistakes? This is a perfect time to take advantage of the fact. Instagram -- a photo-only sharing app at the time and Vine -- a video-only sharing app are perfect examples of being social media competitors. When Vine was introduced to the world, it allowed users to post 6-second videos. Vine went viral and instantly got onto Instagram's radar. Not too long after, Instagram introduced a video sharing feature that allowed up to 15 seconds. Although it didn't put Vine out of business, Instagram made the perfect move to integrate video sharing onto their app. Had they not, Instagram would have lost many users to Vine.

## Instagram Marketing 202

Earlier, I mentioned that Instagram gets its own section because I strongly believe in the power of using Instagram to boost your brand's exposure, gain leads and convert people into customers.

Instagram allows you to upload a photo or a video which will be available to millions of daily active users. All in a small square. You are not allowed to post links in post captions which discourages spammers from posting their link everywhere. Because of that, Instagram encourages genuine users to engage in your content.

People can get lost in time while using Instagram. Being exclusive with full functionality on mobile with the exception of limited desktop use, it can be an easy way to get pulled into Instagram. With a compelling way to "like" a photo by two taps on a screen, an Instagrammer is more likely to engage in a brand's Instagram post compared to a Facebook or Twitter. You can see it for yourself. Compare your friend's Instagram posts to their Facebook posts and see which one has more likes. Most of the time, their photo on Instagram will have more likes than their post on Facebook.

A study by Forrester, a market research company, discovered that Instagram drives 58 times more user engagement than Facebook and 120 times more than Twitter. Looking at six other social media platforms, user engagement was only 0.1%. Instagram had

4.21%. The numbers don't lie. Instagram is far superior in cultivating user engagement and it is the perfect opportunity for you to take advantage of that.

The nature of Instagram calls for users to have an eye for visually pleasing content. Human beings are highly visual. Instagram is highly visual. Many Instagram users crave to share what kind of food they're eating for lunch, where they went for vacation, interesting things that happened to them, funny pictures and beautiful photography. The list goes on and on. Celebrities and Influencers take advantage of Instagram to spread awareness. At times, a celebrity can have more than a million "followers" and when they upload a photo at the tap of the screen, a million people are able to see it. Yelp does a phenomenal job of using Instagram. Yelp being Yelp, food lovers everywhere love using the app to find the newest hotspots. What does Yelp do on their Instagram? You guessed right. They post visually appealing photos of food. The possibilities on Instagram are endless.

When you use Instagram, you can

- **Drive brand awareness** -- An essential part of business. It's easy for users to get to your photo or page through friend like page, the Explore page system, tagging system, and hashtags

- **Show brand transparency** -- Your photos can provide insight into who you are behind your brand name. It allows users to connect with you instead of a faceless corporation. This cultivates trust and builds a relationship.

- **Engage personally** -- Instagram has a unique commenting system in which you have to tag someone to reply to them. It gives a more personal feel to your reply. You can also use strategies that utilize Call to Actions, which compel users to take action and buy your product. Stick with me, I'll explain in a little bit.

- **Convert users into customers** -- having remarkable content with a combination of "call to actions" that drive people to your site will make it more likely for them to convert into customers.

Combine the precedence of millions of young millennial Instagrammers with startups -- a younger demographic and you have your bread and butter.

Before we dive into tapping into the power Instagram, we need a plan. Fortunately, I've got the plan and the fact that you are reading this right now shows that you are ready to learn it.

Let's go.

Our plan is based on three foundations:

**Content**
**Delivery**
**Interaction**

Getting the hang of these three will allow you to use the power of Instagram to better your business than ever before.

**Content**

Your content is what you upload and share with the world. If you are trying to find the type of content you should post, it helps to begin by going into the mind of your audience. Research them. Think about the type of things they would like to see coming from a brand like yours. Are you a clothing brand? It'd be nice to push content that has to do with fashion or the latest trends. Are you a marketing consultant company? Uploading pictures of tips or marketing tricks would attract the type of audience you want. Put yourself in their shoes then think about what they would want to see. Give them a reason to follow you to keep up with the content you are posting.

An important thing to keep in mind when thinking about your content is to keep putting out **valuable content.** Gary Vaynerchuck tries to drill this into the minds of everyone. He says that you should "give value, give value, give value, then ask for business." In the eyes of the people, if you keep giving out valuable content for free, they would be inclined to follow you so they keep gaining knowledge. Then it would be hard to say "no" when you do ask for their business because you have already established that you know what you are talking about and that they do have something to gain from paying for your product or service.

You don't have to pay a celebrity to put out amazing content. This is why I stress the importance of social media marketing. Anyone can become a viral sensation literally overnight. You just have to find the right content.

In my own case, my audience are entrepreneurs and startups. As you already know, marketing is one of the most important things to them. Aside from marketing, entrepreneurs and startups need to possess an extraordinary amount of self-discipline, dedication, a clear mind in the face of failure and the never-ending thirst for knowledge. Their mind is one of their biggest assets. That is why I post what will be important to them and provide value which is motivational and inspirational content with a mix of marketing strategies that they can practically use the very same day. I want my content to be inspirational and useful to everyone who comes across it.

My daily posts provide a boost of inspiration to people who might need a "pick-me-up" or a reminder that the struggles they are currently going through will be worth it. Maybe they  need some marketing tips to gain exposure and build their brand. They can get both of those from my content and the value that I hope to bring is exactly what pulls people in. For me, I am not uploading just for the sake of it. I personally relate to the content which is why I love putting a part of myself out there for the world to see and learn from.

It is important to keep in mind that because Instagram is a highly visual platform, you should put in an effort to make your content look high quality and professional. By this, I mean using the best resolution size for your photo, using beautiful background images, using appealing font and branding your photos. Have an eye for beautiful design. This doesn't mean you have to go out there and paint the next Mona Lisa. Something as simple as using those points I mentioned can result in something people want to look at. Take a look at some of the biggest Instagram accounts of your industry to see what they're doing right. Now put your own spin on it.

A couple of tools and websites I use to create my content:

- Free, no copyright, Hi-Res stock photos: Unsplash.com, Pexels.com
- Photo Creator: Canva.com, Photoshop, Pic-Lab

The bottom line is to make beautiful and valuable content that will pull in viewers.

## Delivery

Delivery is about putting out content on a **consistent schedule** that will maximize your amount of exposure with each post. Building an expectation with your audience that you will repeatedly be uploading valuable content will keep them coming back for more. It also builds anticipation and we both know how important that is. Doing a great job on delivery will allow you to attract more users and better retain the users you already have based on trust that you will keep providing value to them.

So how do we deliver?

The biggest part of delivery is having a consistent posting schedule that you must stick to maximize your exposure. To build the best posting schedule, you have to **look at the best timing to post.**

There is a sea of content that is constantly bombarding everyone's Instagram feeds every single moment of the day. It is important to find the timing so you are the one who gets your content onto their feed at the right time. The best time to post on weekdays is usually in the morning (before everyone starts their day), afternoon (lunch break), and evening (everyone is winding down). On weekends, it can get a little trickier.

Here is my posting schedule I found that works best for me. It is in Pacific Standard Time (PST).

**Monday:** 10am, 1pm, 7pm.
**Tuesday:** 10am 3pm. 7pm.
**Wednesday:** 11am, 1pm, 7pm.
**Thursday:** 10am, 1pm, 9pm.
**Friday:** 1pm, 4pm, 7pm.
**Saturday:** 10am, 3pm, 8pm.
**Sunday:** 11am, 3pm, 10pm.

Using this posting schedule allows me to gain the most interaction from users. Something to keep in mind is that "prime-time" is usually in the evening which is the last time frame I listed each day. People want to unwind from the events of the day so they like to go on their Instagram feeds to see what's new.

**IMPORTANT:** Do not send a hailstorm of posts all at once. This can make your account look like an advertisement account instead of having a genuine touch. What is ideal is to post three to four times a day all spaced out using your posting schedule.

**Interact**

Now that you have valuable content with consistent delivery, you should be building an audience. The next step is to interact or engage with your audience using call-to-actions. Call-to-actions are instructions that encourage user engagement. This can drive more exposure through likes, comments, shares and tags or bigger things like encouragement to buy your product or signing up to your email list. It can come in many forms but for the purpose of Instagram, it is something much more simple and creative.

Almost everything you post should give people the opportunity for engagement.

The simplest way to do this is to use the actual photo as a call-to-action or to use your description as a place to put it. Be mindful of how your audience feels by how much you are asking. With the simpler things I just mentioned, you can do it on almost every photo. But with other things like asking them to buy your product or giving their email to you, you have to be mindful of how much times you are asking. The best way to use bigger call-to-action tactics like those is to first build a relationship and trust *then* ask.

Some of the best call-to-actions are the simplest ones:

Tag someone you know who…
Double tap if you agree!
Posing a question
Present a small challenge or contest

I find that using these simple ones do drive user engagement more than not using them.

Keep in mind that it is not forcing someone to do something. People should enjoy and want to double tap like or tag their friend. This goes back to providing valuable content that they feel relates to them.

**QUICK TIP:**

Use the description box to drive even more user engagement. Provide one or three sentences that further explain the photo you posted. It gives more of a human feel behind the post which further cultivates trust. After your description, don't forget to put a simple call-to-action.

**ANOTHER QUICK TIP:**

Use hashtags. They make your content easier to find for people who don't follow you. It groups your photos together and creates a more targeted audience. Figure out the most important hashtags to your industry. The way I use hashtags is by posting another comment separately from my description.

Using bullet points before you type your hashtags will make your comment section look more sleek. Take a look at this:

- 
- 
- 
- 

#hashtags #inspiration #theartofmarketing
#thankyouforreadingthisfar #youareawesome

This makes it so your description and comment section isn't filled with hashtags at a first glance. It cleans up your comment section.

You can use up to 30 hashtags per post so make sure to take advantage of that!

**Blogging**

Say the word "blog" five times in a row. Blog blog blog blog blog. It starts to sound weird right? It makes you question what the word actually means.

So what is blogging?

Blogging is a tried and true method of gaining traffic by educating your viewers, entertaining them or just providing something relevant to them. They are written posts and they usually aren't very long -- they are meant to be quick and easy to read or view. It is shorter than an ebook but still provides valuable information. It solves their needs whether it is a how-to article or an inspiring story that makes them want to do something they've never done before.

It is important to write blog posts about content relating to your business or niche. If you were in a business that sells men's suits, it would be a good idea to write about the do's and don'ts of wearing a suit. If you had an eCommerce business that creates custom designs, it is a good idea to write about the different types of designs or to educate the public on the art of your craft. This shows people that you are very knowledgeable in your field and that gives them just another reason they should trust you.

The best thing about blogging is that it is very good at driving traffic to your site. That provides an opportunity for people to be converted into customers. If this happens, blogging has helped you achieve your goal.

Each time you create a blog post, it gives your website more of a chance to be listed in Google's search. This is very important because anyone that has ever had access to the internet has used Google search.

BuzzFeed, the internet media company that has uploaded many viral content in the past and counting, does a phenomenal job of content marketing. Though they don't actually aim to sell a product, their enormous multimillion following gives an incentive for advertisers to pay for ad space. BuzzFeed then features them in some way that doesn't make it seem like advertising to the common user. Genius.

If you want to grow your personal brand like my friend, Tam Pham, you can also accomplish that by blogging. Tam left school to pursue his own dreams of helping people learn what they actually need to succeed in life. Tam has his own blog, OutsideoftheClassroom, centered on providing alternatives to a college education and providing guidance and tools to people who are going down the same path as himself. His blog features topics such as career, business, motivation and life. Tam knows why people come to his site and he creates content that will provide enough value to them to go out and pursue their own dreams. He uses strategies such as building an email list, creating podcasts and providing users incentives to learn from his Amazon Bestseller book, *How to Network.* If you'd like to check out what Tam has in store for you, you can visit his site at outsideoftheclassroom.com.

## How to Get Started On Blogging

Now that we understand the basics of blogging, we can put this strategy into action. To set up a blog, WordPress  has made it quick and easy whether you are trying to build your personal brand as an entrepreneur, startup or trying to grow your small business.

Certainly, you can set up a blog in just a couple of moments by yourself. If you feel you aren't capable of creating a professionally designed website and need some help, you can outsource it to someone who can professionally build it for you if you had the funds. I want to teach you how to do it on your own as seamlessly as possible.

Many people like to use WordPress to create their website and set up their own blog because it allows them to create both in the same place. It is easy to set up, manage and update. While it is true that it started out as a blogging system, it has also turned its sails to accomodate website creation. Head over to WordPress , create your account and it should guide you through the steps to create your website!

**Looks Do Matter**

Now, the website is something that people will base your image off as long as they can see it. It is important to choose a professionally designed theme that you can install onto your website! Remember, people are highly visual so it is a good decision to create a visually appealing website. While Uber, Airbnb and Apple probably hired web developers to custom create their site, both of them are great examples of visually stunning websites. They feature sitewide cover photos with an overlay of words. They are also minimalistic which drives user retention and makes it easy for users to navigate. Lucky for you, there are many themes on WordPress that resemble them. Choose one that shows people that you are the real deal.

**Types of Content You Can Create**

So you've set up your website and you are ready to start creating content that will be valuable to people. Looks like we're off to a great start. There are many types of content you can create. While you don't have to create all of them, it is a good idea to start and focus on one in the beginning. Some examples include:

- **Blog posts.** This is what blogging is centered around. Written posts that provide value to people by teaching them something or being relevant to them.

- **Infographics.** If you are talented at graphic design, creating an infographic is a great way to catch the attention of people. They are also more likely to be shared on social media. Using well-researched information, you can create one that teaches people something just by having them look at it.

- **Podcasts.** A podcast is a video or audio recording that people can download to and listen in the moment or at a later time. You can use this opportunity to educate your viewers by speaking which gives it a more human touch.

- **Ebooks.** These are great for packing in a lot of information to educate anyone who reads them. They are great incentives for people to sign up to your email list (something I will talk about soon).

- **Videos.** We've talked about the relevance of YouTube  and you can embed videos from your YouTube channel to be directly viewed on your site.

- **Photos.** Going back to the notion that people are highly visual beings, photos are a great way to break up a wall of text and provide a different dynamic of life to your website.

I recommend just starting on blog posts in the beginning, but if you have talent in creating any other type of content, you know which one you are comfortable in choosing.

**Ways to Get Traffic**

**1. Influencers**
Back to the idea of utilizing the power of Influencers and the enormous amount of exposure they can bring with them, they are a great asset to any blog no matter the size or following. If you really want to get more exposure, they are one of the major keys. Having an influencer in your industry write for you will provide you with great content and drive your traffic and exposure through their massive following. Sounds like a good idea.

Of course, if you are just starting out, you wouldn't have too much incentives to offer... or do you?
Here are two of the best things you can offer to influencers:

- **Free access to your product or service.** Who doesn't like free things? Giving your product to them for free is going to be a very powerful incentive to get them to create content for you. Bonus points if you have a product that will solve their need.

- **A link that directs viewers back to their own website.** This will drive viewers from your own blog back to their website. Essentially, they will gain even more viewers just by writing a guest post for your blog. More viewers is something they want. Give it to them.

Remember, don't just go straight for pitching an email to them. With influencers, it is important to build a relationship with them and then ease into providing an opportunity that benefit both of you. If you need a reminder on Influencers, you can go back to the Power of the People chapter and review the Influencer section to get a quick refresher.

**Guest post**

Writing guest posts for popular blogs is a great way of gaining more exposure. Reaching out to others in your industry can help you quickly build a name for your brand. If you could tap into a popular blog with a massive following, you can build your email list subscriptions (I will talk about your email list soon) and get a couple thousand more pair of eyes that now know your business.

When trying to find a blog to guest post, you can Google (*your industry* + guest post) and a ton of sites that are open to receiving guest posts will appear. Make sure to check how big their following is by going onto their blog and seeing the amount of engagement they receive. Some sites have a list of guest blogs and provide information about their engagement so you can choose each one accordingly.

Also, using the website, Help A Reporter Out, can give you many opportunities to help reporters write a post. Often, reporters are required to meet a specific quota and they need help finding the next biggest ideas. They will often pitch a topic with instructions on what they want to see from potential guest writers.

Once you've found the one you want to guest post for, take a look at their guidelines for guest post submissions. If they don't have an option for guest posting, look around and do some research to whether they are open for business. Leaving many thoughtful comments on the blog so they can get to know you is a good way to get your foot in the door. Then you could send an email pitch to them providing your information and several ideas that you believe are potential posts with valuable content for their readers. See if they reply and proceed with their instructions.

It is not the end of the world if they don't reply. At times, the most popular blogs have a massive amount of requests a day and they can take quite a while to respond or even not at all. That's okay, move on and keep trying.

The results you can get with guest blogging are phenomenal. First and foremost, you get more exposure and traffic. Secondly, you can get a massive increase in email list subscriptions. Third, you are able to build a relationship with other bloggers in your industry and you add another reputable item to yourself or your business.

**Sharing more than once**
I often see others doing this and it goes to say that people will see your post more compared to sharing it just once and forgetting about it. They will often share

their post across all of their social media platforms, repeat the same thing just on one of two platforms the following day and then share it again on all platforms the next week. This helps get their post in front of people that otherwise might not have seen it and shows that their post still matters. It is important to keep in mind that you should always be smart about spacing out your posts. This is one of the best ways to avoid spamming everyone's newsfeeds. A great reposting schedule would look like the following:

- **Initial post**

- **Next Day**

- **Next Week**

- **Next Month**

- **Next 3 months and beyond**

Once you've set up a great reposting schedule, it is very important to remember to add variety to your posts. Adding variety means not posting the same message each time. Here are a few examples that I have seen others doing:

- **Basic** - title, caption and link

- **Quotes** - a sentence from the blog

- **Cite a fact** - something that will make people say "wow" or react

- **Ask a question** - This can stir up a conversation

After you've set up a great reposting schedule while switching up each individual message, you should keep in mind the feedback that you are receiving. Are the number of clicks/views going up or is it staying the same? Are there negative comments?

You are probably worried that people might see you coming off as spammy but the truth is that people rarely care when you are actually providing valuable information instead of a horde of advertisements. However, it is possible to go over the line. I believe if you were to try this strategy, it would be smart to start slow -- publish the initial post and then republish the following week then work your way up.

**Search Engine Optimization (SEO)**

Using SEO and keywords can drive big time traffic to your blog or website. From optimizing the words in your posts, people can find what they are searching the web for easily. So why do you need SEO? Well, the majority of traffic on the web is driven by search engines like Google and Bing. Yes, it is true that a great amount of your traffic can come from social media and other outlets, but there is a significant amount of traffic that can come from powerful search engines.

Look at it this way. Someone is trying to find a way to send money to their family overseas. Right now, that person is trying to find information on how to do that and so they search for "send money overseas" in Google. They are hungry. Your startup is a payment centered company that is able to do accommodate their needs. You have the plate of food they want but you need to find the best way to get that plate of food in front of them. Having the right keywords that match what that person is searching will give you a higher chance of popping up on Google's search results -- and thus having them click on your link and going to your website. They choose you to provide them a way to send money to their family overseas and you just got a new customer. Search engines provide targeted traffic. They are actively looking for what you can offer. Go ahead, try it out. The first few results are generally the ones that people most often click on. Search up "send money overseas" and in the first few results, you can spot the payment processing company, PayPal. They've done SEO and you should too.

**The Basics of SEO**

SEO can be split into two parts: Research and optimizing.

Research means finding the right keywords to utilize. You usually want to find keywords that have:

- **High search volume**
- **Low competition**
- **Relevant to your content**

You can use the most popular tool to find them, Google Keyword Planner.

But first, I must talk about *long tail keywords*. They are essentially a chain of low traffic keywords that can combine to form most of your traffic. They can be used with single, high traffic keywords to put your site higher up in the search rankings.

The best way to find long tail keywords is to:

1. Do a simple Google Search of your topic and look at the search suggestions box

2. Write down some of those.

3. Take a look at the related search suggestions at the bottom of the page. Write down some of those too.

4. Enter those terms into Google Keywords and see their statistics.

5. Try to find ones that have the highest traffic and the lowest competition.

6. Repeat with finding the best single keywords

7.  Once you've found the best terms, you can add them into your content to optimize!

**IMPORTANT:** Here is something to keep in mind. You should NOT be writing your content just for search engine optimization. This will throw off the natural feel to your content. Focus on writing great quality content and then add some optimized keywords. Try to find the best balance between the both.

**And a quick tip:** If you want to see how well your website is set up, you can use HubSpot's Website Grader. It tests the strength of your website ranging from performance loading times, SEO, mobile optimization and security. It is a great way to discover mistakes in your website so you can fix them. It is important to construct your website as strong as it can be to improve user interaction through performance, get more traffic through mobile and search engine optimization as well as increasing revenue.

**Building A Content Funnel**

So now you've gotten traffic coming to your website or blog from using the techniques we've just talked about. What do we do now? Well, you didn't know it at first but when you were creating valuable content, you were also making the first part of a *content funnel*. A content funnel lays out the process that people go through when they visit your site. It helps organize their experience from initially coming to your site to them purchasing your product. It helps you prevent losing potential customers who otherwise might have just left your site after reading a few articles.

Imagine an actual funnel that is is split into 3 parts: top, middle and bottom.

At the top, you have a bigger opening that catches the attention of people. They might be visiting your site for the first time by stumbling on your link or seeing your website in the search engines. The goal in this stage isn't to sell to them. The goal in this stage is to build trust and establish a relationship with them.

You can build a relationship by:

- **Content. Content. Content.**
Putting out valuable content that shows them that you know what you are talking about and that they have things they can learn from you. You'll be seen as a source of information and not someone just someone trying to sell right off the bat.

**and then...**

- **Email Subscription List**
Encouraging them to subscribe to your email list will allow them to keep up to date with what's going on in your business. The email list is a great place to provide even more valuable information that is exclusive only to them. Offering something for free, like an ebook or free

tool, is a very effective way of encouraging people to provide you with their email.

At the middle, you've gotten people that are interested in what you have to say and they've given you their email and contact information in exchange for a source of great information. Don't bombard them with sales pitches and advertisements in this stage. Instead, encourage them to sign up for maybe a free trial to your product or something to capture their attention at the end of one of your top posts. Here, the goal is to keep nurturing your relationship with them. After all, they've taken the time to subscribe to your email list and they should receive exclusive content that isn't available to the public. Keep providing relevant information to them so they can keep learning what you know or send them the ebook you promised them. Also, you can encourage them to reply to you so they feel they have a voice to get any of their questions answered. It is crucial to treat your email list subscribers with care as they have some kind of interest invested in you already and you don't want to lose them.

The bottom of the funnel is where your readers and audience have the highest potential to purchase your product. At this point, they are highly invested in you and they are ready to make the exchange. You've become a trusted source of information to them and they've shown they want to proceed further either by signing up to your product or wanting to get in touch with you. That's great!

As you can see, using a content funnel is a great way to acquire more customers. It captures their attention and guides them through the process to purchasing your product. It is a great way to build a relationship with them, nurture that relationship and at the end, if they feel you are fit to solve their problems and needs, they will purchase your product.

# Events

Events are a great way for your startup or business to gain a significant amount of exposure to a targeted audience. After all, they have chosen to attend the event to find more about the organizations that are going to be there. Put yourself in front of them and you will find people who have a problem or need -- and you are going to be the one to help them solve that.

Hustle Con is an annual one-day event for non-technical startup founders looking for in-depth information presented by speakers who have been in their shoes. It is a great event to learn about the highs and lows of having a startup and practical advice you could use the very same day. At the event, there are tons of like-minded entrepreneurs, startup founders, and investors who attend. Some notable speakers in the past include successful startup founders like Tim Westergren (Pandora), Walker Williams (Teespring) and Arum Kang (Coffee Meets Bagel). What do you get in a room full of people looking to network and help each other grow their business? Growth. Exposure. Knowledge. Support. All things you want and need in the field of entrepreneurship.

Another similar event is Startup Weekend which is a three-day event that encompasses networking, discovery, knowledge and practical steps to get started on implementing what you have learned during your time there. There are many notable startups that attend like Swipes and Rover that pass on their knowledge so you can grow your business.

These are just two examples of how attending an event will grant you more knowledge than you've ever had before, building your brand awareness and connecting with like-minded entrepreneurs who possess the ambition to succeed in this difficult pathway of life. Who knows, you can find someone to invest in your business or someone who possesses extraordinary skills who wants to work for you. You will also definitely find similar movers and shakers that are in the same boat as you. You will definitely learn. You will definitely grow.

Try to search for events you can attend that allow you to set up a booth or pitch to potential investors. Startup Weekend gives attendees 60 seconds to pitch their startup to the thousands in the audience. Talk about exposure. Having your logo displayed to thousands and thousands of people will definitely increase your brand awareness by providing information to attendees and answering their questions. Combine that with an exceptional product that solves a need and you will be successful.

# Leverage Your Network

*"Give me a place to stand, and a lever long enough, and I will move the world. " - Archimedes*

Archimedes got the idea. Using leverage is a very powerful asset you can utilize in your business. Entrepreneurs are often told "if you want something done right... do it yourself". There is some truth in that only if you are able to do it yourself because you are an expert on it or have the time and resources to accomplish it. However, smart entrepreneurs will find ways to leverage the skills, abilities, time and resources of others who can either do it better than themselves or to optimize efficiency. There is simply an insane amount of tasks and to-do's to be done in such a short amount of time that getting a little help for certain things can pay dividends in the long run. Having someone to help you on a task so you can focus more time on things you are an expert on will instantly improve how your business is doing. There is a constant debate between "working hard" and "working smart" and in the end, it is the combination of both that will bring you further than where you've ever been before. In having a startup or being an entrepreneur, it is extremely crucial to work smart because you would want to get the most out of every minute of work you put in. Entrepreneurs simply need to do more with less.  It is also extremely important to work hard but when you combine working hard and working smart, you will get the most out of everything that you do. In business, it is all about building relationships with people and to treat them like actual human beings instead of cold pitching your product right off the bat. When you use leverage, it is a two-sided benefit to both parties involved. This being said, you should never take advantage of someone just because you can. It is all about being ethical.

We've already talked about using leverage before in the form of getting traffic through blogging. Strategies such as guest posting and building relationships with influencers are both forms of leverage. You are benefitting from their already established audience and they are getting valuable content to post for their readers. Groove, the online support system "help desk" startup, used leverage to spread brand awareness to millions of people by tapping into another startup, Buffer. By being able to guest post on Buffer's blog, they gained a tremendous amount of exposure in a short amount of time. In one post, Groove received more subscribers to their email list than two or even three of their own posts on their own blog combined.

The best entrepreneurs are great in networking and in networking with others, they are able to do more with less. Networking is a powerful tool but there is a fine line in it. Do it right and you will find yourself doing better than ever before with the amount of resources available to you. Do it wrong and the only relationships you'll be making are bad ones. Tam Pham states in his Amazon Bestseller book, *How To Network: Build Instant Trust & Respect With Anyone You Meet,* that "networking = making friends. Think of networking like making friends." Having the right mindset that networking is making friends will take you a long way. You wouldn't treat your friends like a piece of meat would you? A friendship is all about mutual respect. Tam also mentions the Silver Bullet which is the idea that the best thing you can give someone is ideas. Give, give, give and you shall receive. Never expect anything in return. In giving someone valuable ideas, a relationship can be built on the exchange of knowledge which will benefit everyone in the end. The moral of the story is to make friends!

Aside from forms of leverage for building relationships and gaining exposure, there is another way of using leverage to improve the efficiency of your business. This is by getting time to be on your side because as we know, there are too many tasks to be done and not enough time. Even with amazing prioritization skills, a person in the nature of building a startup or being an entrepreneur cannot do it all by herself. They need help. They need to find others who can do the job better than them or someone to help them save exponential time. A great way to find help is to find freelancers who are willing to provide their skills, time and resources in exchange for compensation or some other form of reimbursement. By hiring freelancers, there is less costs involved as compared to a full-time employee. Freelancers don't receive medical, dental or other benefits. As a startup, it is important to remember that this saves tremendously on your cash flow while still receiving great help from qualified freelancers. This may come as a surprise, but Uber drivers are not full time employees of Uber. Uber claims that their drivers are hired as freelancers. Uber, now a multimillion company, uses a different kind of business model by hiring their drivers as freelancers. The nature of their product enables them to operate this way. By having freelancers, you don't have to worry about keeping them after the project is finished because being freelancers, they will move on to another project after. However, there are always cases where freelancers believe working for a certain business is a great fit for them and they want to become long time partners. If a startup is successful enough, they will eventually hire full-time employees. This a great sign! No matter if they are a freelancer or employee, always treat them with respect. One of my favorite notions is that you should treat the janitor with the same level of respect as the CEO.

The bottom line with using leverage is to do more with less, work smart AND work hard and make friends.

# Pricing Strategy

As an entrepreneur, you need to find out the best pricing model for your products in a market where there haven't been past standards to learn from. Price too little and you leave money on the table, price too much and you will lose potential customers. The best businesses will use pricing to their advantage to reinforce their value and the message they hope to send. There are many types of pricing strategies out there, but I will touch on the ones that I believe are best for entrepreneurs because of their simplicity and effectiveness. One quick thing to mention about pricing is that it is very psychological. At times, people can perceive pricing to be the deciding factor if they choose to buy your product or to move on and find another alternative. When you spot products being sold with a dollar amount ending in ".99", ".97", or ".50", it is not an accident. There are sound psychological reasons business price their products this way and when you find out the reason behind that, you are more knowledgeable in pricing your own products as well as seeing why other businesses are conducting their pricing strategy this way. Before we begin, it is very important to consider your business' value, positioning and message. Companies like Apple can charge an extraordinary amount for their products because of their prestige and reputation. On the other hand, Samsung is a competitor to Apple but must price their products at a lower rate because well, they're not Apple. If your business sends a message that your products provide an advantage in the economy, then your prices are going to be competitive. However, if your brand's message has to do with luxury, then you must price your products higher because who wants to pay for a luxury item that doesn't cost much? This goes back to the fact that pricing is psychological. Expensive = good. When done right, it can raise the perceived value of the product even if the product stays the same. Imagine if Apple sold their new iPhones for less than $50?

One of my favorite strategies is the Price Anchoring Strategy. At its core it is offering different versions of your product at different prices. This strategy adds a ton of value to your brand by offering multiple prices to your product that can work in conjunction with each other to maximize your revenue and provide great options and alternatives to potential customers. While the price anchoring strategy works best for subscription business models, it can also be applied to products such as cologne bottle sizes for example.

**However, subscription type services are great for three reasons:**

1. It creates flexibility and balance by offering a different array of pricing plans that benefit different types of users and the business by being able to accommodate a variety of people.

2. They are more reliable as customers have a recurring payment plan. Subscribers never have to

remember to reorder the product in case they run out. It runs on the idea of simplicity and automation.

3. Allows a business to easier predict annual revenue through recurring sales

Subscription pricing is great for product and SaaS (software as a service) businesses but what about service businesses? According to Chuck Longanecker, founder of Digital Telepathy, when he switched his business model to subscription type only, he found a 300% increase in annual revenue. Instead of having customers being billed for pay-per-service, he completely restructured it to subscription type only. It allowed his business to work in alignment with their goals such as having flexibility in their types of services, reliability for customers knowing the service is on call, and stronger relationships with customers over time because they are subscribed to their services. If you don't have a subscription type pricing model, consider the pros and cons of switching over for your particular situation. It can pay off in the long run.

A crucial component of subscription pricing models is the ability to anchor your prices. By using the price anchoring strategy, you can make a certain option more appealing because people have the choice to weigh their options.

To explain what I'm talking about, here is an example of a good price anchoring strategy:

Premium: $599.99/month
Value: $199.99/month
Basic: $99.99/month

As you can see here, the Premium plan is extremely more expensive than the Value or Basic plans. This is on purpose. The Premium plan may have the best exclusive features that considerably less people would purchase. However, these are the more serious users who absolutely need the features that come with the Premium plan. The goal with the Premium plan is not to sell the most quantity. The real goal with Premium is to make the Value plan look more appealing. Psychologically, most people are thinking that with the Premium plan, they don't need all the features that come with it and it's a little extreme in pricing so it's not the one they will choose. When they take a look at the Value plan, they see that it provides all the services they need without the extra exclusive features of Premium. They also see that it's cost effective as compared to the Premium plan and provides more than the Basic plan, so they will choose to buy the Value Plan. The goal here is to focus on sales with the majority of the Value plan with less people buying the Basic or Premium plan. If people do buy the Premium plan, well, that's just another bonus to the business.

Another way to do this is to change the presentation of the prices:

Value: $19.99/month
Premium: $39.99/month
Annual Premium: $399.99/year

Here, I've added an annual plan for Premium that is considerably less than the monthly plan for Premium if a person bought it for the whole year with the monthly purchases instead of paying it all at once. The monthly Premium plan would come out to $479.88/year while the annual Premium plan would be $399.99/year. People would think that by buying the Premium monthly plan, they are getting as much as they could out of that plan for the best price. People also try to avoid paying extreme amounts all at once, so if they really need the Premium service but don't want to buy the annual version of it, they would pay more over the course of the year. The goal of the annual Premium plan is to make the Premium plan look more appealing because of its low monthly cost.

Webydo, the website creator that allows users to create websites without coding, utilizes a very effective pricing strategy:

Pro: $90/month,
Team: $180/month
Agency: $480/month

You can see that Agency plan is way more expensive than the other two. However, the Agency plan provides many exclusive features. While the monthly version plans are billed on a monthly basis and you could unsubscribe at anytime, they are more expensive as compared to the annual plans which comes at a discount of 20% off each month but billed all at once for the year. Webydo is able to provide flexibility for a variety of users, build stronger relationships by retaining users and have a steady incoming cash flow by using price anchoring and a subscription type pricing model.

Robert Cialdini in his book, *Influence: The Psychology of Persuasion,* explains this psychological phenomenon as the contrast principle. He states that "the contrast principle affects the way we see the difference between two things that are presented one after another". Now that you know about the contrast principle, you can spot it in many areas of everyday life. Even in restaurants like McDonalds, you can see that they price their 20-piece chicken nuggets at $4.99 and their 10-piece chicken nuggets at $4.29. The majority of people would buy the 20 piece for $4.99 because it's only 70 cents more and you get double the 10 piece nuggets! That is exactly what McDonalds wants.

# Marketing Plan

So now after we've went over all these strategies and tactics you could use in your marketing, it is a good idea to organize everything so we have a clear idea for what we are going to do. After all, execution is one the most important steps of startups. If you have the greatest idea but you never make it happen, it's not going to do anything to benefit you. Having a plan will help you organize everything so you know what resources to spend and when to spend them. In the long run, it reduces the stress of marketing and the weight on your business altogether. You will know your next move. You will know when to execute your next move. The nature of being in entrepreneurship means you have so much to do and such little time. A million things are running through your head and it really does help to make a plan and organize your strategies. A marketing plan won't guarantee you success, but it will greatly increase your chances of it. I promise that.

Let's get started on crafting our plan.

First off, in the nature of startups and entrepreneurship, everything is moving at a lightning fast pace. It is redundant to have a long term marketing strategy that runs over a year. Things change and startups need to constantly adjust their plan to appeal to the ever-changing market. One of my favorite quotes sums this up perfectly:

*"No plan of operations extends with certainty beyond the first encounter with the enemy's main strength."* - *Helmuth Karl Bernhard Graf von Moltke*

Moltke was a Prussian military strategist and even if I can't pronounce his whole name, I believe this quote by him is brilliant. In plain English, it means that no plan survives the first encounter with the enemy. This is because even if you can create a beautifully crafted plan, unexpected events always come up that force you to change your original plan. In a startup, there is not enough time and resources to have a concrete plan in the present to optimize your chance of success. This isn't an attack on having long-term plans; it is necessary to have concrete goals you want to achieve in the long term. Remember, there are always two sides to everything. It just means that you have to change your strategies and tactics to get to those goals. This is why I believe having a plan up to 3 months in advance is a great point between the two sides. Think back about where you were two weeks ago. If you've been reading this far, you probably learned a lot more about marketing (I hope) than you did before picking this book up. Now if you already have a business, think back two or three weeks back. In that short amount of time, things can and have probably changed. In short, what we need to do is craft a simple marketing plan.

In our marketing plan, we will split it into four parts:
**Goals, Strategies, Execution** and **Review/Analyze.**

I will be using my experience of being the Marketing
Director of Peerbuds to help you see the strategies in
action and that I'm not just throwing around nonsense
ideas.

**Goals**
By now, you should have identified your target market
and decided on what you can do to solve their need.
What are you trying to achieve right now? Are you
trying to acquire more customers? Build your social
media presence? Are you trying to spread brand
awareness? Put your long-term goals to the side right
now. What is your purpose in the short term?

During our launch here at Peerbuds, our goal was to
acquire 10 tutors and 20 students who would be our
first group of users. Although it doesn't sound like too
much people, we wanted to start small in a certain
niche. Before expanding to encompass a platform that
allows anyone to teach anything, we wanted to start in
an academic niche. These tutors would be experts in
teaching calculus, physics, biology, chemistry and
accounting. The students would be people struggling
and need personalized 1-on-1 help in these subjects.
Our goal was just to have a balance of tutors to
students for this early stage. Along with acquiring these
30 users, our other goals were to establish a social
media presence and focus on specific high school and
university campuses all across California. The

overarching goal here was to focus on a small niche and dominate it.

Here are four criteria for your goals:

**Be Specific.** Your goals need to be specific. Write them down somewhere. Write them down on paper. Write them down on a whiteboard. Write them on a poster you can hang up in your office or somewhere you can easily see them.

**Measurable.** How do you know how close you are to achieving these goals? They should be measurable meaning they should have a quantity to them. There are a few exceptions but try to get as specific as you can by being measurable.

**Realistic.** I know, this goes against the "spirit of an entrepreneur" but setting realistic goals you can achieve in a short amount of time will set you up for success in the long run. Wanting to be the next Apple in 3 short months is highly unlikely. It can be discouraging. Aim high but not high enough that you can't shoot that far.

**Time.** Time is so important. For your goals, they need to have a deadline. Three months is a great timeline. Not too long, not too short.

**Strategies**

Your goals are what you want to achieve. Your strategies/tactics are the means you are going to take to achieve them. How will you do it? What growth hacks can you come up with and use? What social media platforms are you going to use? Are you going to use a blog to take advantage of SEO and pull in users?

To make it easier to remember and visualize, I laid out the past strategies that we've went through:

**Content Marketing:** blogs, website, infographics, email campaigns, etc.
**Social Media Marketing:** Facebook, Instagram, Twitter and their strategies, etc.
**Growth Hack Marketing:** Innovate ways to integrate automatic virality into your product
**Power of the people:** Utilizing your network (influencers, guest posting, being genuine)
**Generating Anticipation:** People want what they can't have
**Events:** Gain a ton of targeted exposure and network
**Pricing Strategy:** Strategically planning prices using psychological concepts

Though it doesn't seem like much when laid out in a list, these strategies dig deep down to tap into the power of marketing. Of course, you are not limited to just these as there is also traditional advertising, for example. Use these wisely and effectively and you will increase your chances of success.

At Peerbuds, to achieve our goal of getting 10 tutors and 20 students, we came up with a great incentive for the first 30 people that sign up that would make a special aura of exclusivity. I gave the idea that we should give the 10 tutors a higher percentage of the session cost for life. Since this was only available to 10 tutors, it would create a sense of urgency AND exclusivity. For the 20 students, they received a voucher for a highly discounted session. Since we wanted to target an academic niche for certain subjects on certain campuses, we left bookmarks on study area tables and flyers around buildings for that specific subject. We also set up a table and used mini-games to attract passing people . For social media, I wanted to improve our image on Facebook and Instagram mainly so I used the strategies I talked about in the Social Media chapter. Since then, we've experienced more than a 200% increase in our social media following by providing valuable and beautiful content to our users.

**Execution**

*"Ideas are sh\*t. Execution is the game." - Gary Vaynerchuk*

Gary Vaynerchuk put this nicely. Once again, you can have the best idea out there but if you don't execute, it's never going to get anywhere. Putting our strategies into action will allow us to take advantage of the tremendous benefits that they bring. Find a way -- any way to make your ideas happen. It doesn't have to be a perfect idea yet to execute, that is why we have a step to reflect and analyze. This is why I want to provide actionable strategies in this book instead of theoretical ones. It should be clear already. Execute.

One crucial thing we knew as a startup at Peerbuds was that we needed time to be on our side. When any of us came up with a great idea, we wanted to execute that idea as soon as we could. One of the best examples of this was when I first became Marketing Director, I worked tirelessly to come up with great growth hack ideas and social media strategies we could utilize. I worked into the night and had a meeting the very next day with Sahil Parekh, our CEO. Sahil then had a meeting with our developers in the next four hours after I told him about my ideas and the developers started working to implement those ideas as fast as they could. This process of relaying ideas from myself to the CEO to the developers took 24 hours. It was a great feeling to see something that I came up with go into action so quick. We wanted to make it happen as fast as we could. We didn't want those ideas to go to waste. We executed.

**Review/Analyze**

This is the whole reason why our plan needs to be short term. As we execute our strategies, we need to take a step back to review the performance of how well we're doing. Using concepts like A/B testing or any analytical tools like Google Analytics or KISSmetrics, it is possible to see the numbers and statistics. Once you review the analytics, determine whether or not you should stay on that path or change courses. Find out whether you are reaching your goals using the strategies you employ. If it's working, that is great! If not, find what went wrong. Are you setting too high for the time being? Are your strategies not working for your particular situation? Find out what went wrong, evaluate and fix it.

At Peerbuds, I initially thought it would be a good idea to give out vouchers in the form of dollars. There was one problem however... Being in the early stages of a startup, we didn't have the money in a dollar amount to give. After having a talk with Sahil, we decided to switch it over to a percentage type voucher. Having the vouchers in the form of percentages meant that we would take a smaller cut in our profit that would be already generated by the session. In the end, we still receive a profit from the exchange and acquire more users. For our social media, I saw that the strategies that were being used were not optimizing the power of social media. I had a talk with the team and showed them an alternate way to go about conducting ourselves online. Of course, as stated earlier, we saw more than a 200% increase in social media following and it is still growing to this day.

*"You must be shapeless, formless, like water. When you pour water in a cup, it becomes the cup. When you pour water in a bottle, it becomes the bottle. When you pour water in a teapot, it becomes the teapot. Water can drip and it can crash. Become like water my friend."*
*- Bruce Lee*

Having flexibility in our plan is so crucial to success. We are able bend and make changes to areas that need improvement. This isn't a biology book but the process of natural selection thrives on adaptability. The ones that can adapt to adversity survive. That is something that separates successful businesses from others.

# Before I Go….

By now, I hope you've learned more about marketing than if you hadn't picked up my book. I don't believe marketing is just about *marketing.* Marketing is a staple in business and being in business pushes you to your limits. It will test your strengths but more importantly, your weaknesses. To be successful in business is to have a strong mindset that stands against the test of failure and to possess the ability to keep going through the hard times. The best traits to possess are having an amazing work ethic, being dedicated to your goals, persevering, and having an open mind to be fueled by inspiration. Those aren't the only things I believe a business owner should have but to me, those are the ones that are crucial to being successful not just in business but in life. Don't be intimidated by the daunting challenges ahead of you. If you are, I am here to tell you that I have been in your position before. I admit that I too, have been scared, been intimidated and been lost. Even to this day, I still feel I am. The only thing that matters when you are unsure of yourself is to keep pushing on. The only way to find out how strong you are is to keep pushing your limits. Business is about having the right mindset. Before I conclude this book, I leave you with a few of my thoughts on being the best version of yourself:

**Be Genuine In All That You Are**

*"Everything I do, I'm a man behind mine" -Jay Z*

Marketing is about the people and in being about the people, it is about being genuine. Having that quality in your character will take you farther in life than you will ever think. When you are genuine in your actions, you never have to worry about hiding something from the public. You will never have to act with an ulterior motive with a smile in the corner of your mouth as you are about to take advantage of someone. Everything you do should be in the best interest of others. Never think you have to screw somebody over in business in order to succeed. Through my experience with others, I have heard too many times that the business world is a dog-eat-dog world. It's not. Too many times I hear of salesmen taking advantage of people who don't know any better and selling them something they don't even need or want. They do it just to make money. To succeed in business, you have to bring each other up. To succeed in life, you cannot throw another person under the bus to get what you want. Don't sacrifice the integrity of your character to make a quick buck. Ask yourself if you would feel good about yourself by taking advantage of another human being. If I cannot do something for someone to the best of my abilities, I will recommend an alternative way to help them-- even if it is not me helping them. When you are truly genuine, people will naturally sense that coming from you. It opens an endless supply of opportunities and opens new doors that wouldn't otherwise be opened. For example, people will feel good about doing business with you and they will recommend you to their friends and family because they trust you. When you genuinely put other people's best interests at the top of your list, you will be at the top of their list.

## Underdogs

Some of my favorite stories are from people who are going through the hardest of times and coming out on the top. They are the underdogs.

Back when I was in high school, I use to run track and field. I ran the hurdles. Now if you have never met me in person, I am going to tell you that I am not tall. I was not "born to run hurdles" while my competitors look like they came straight out of the womb to be athletes. I was not going to let my height be a factor to stop me from going after my dreams. I wanted to achieve my dream of making it to the State Championships by the time I graduated. I was just in my first year of middle school, young and all skin and bones when I set this goal. Since I was at a disadvantage, I had to work harder than others just to be on the same level as my naturally athletic competitors. When I was on the same level as them, I had to sacrifice my free time -- going out with friends and normal things teenagers do, to be on the next level ahead of them. It is in the eerie silence of blood, sweat and tears that success is bred. Day in and day out, I imagined myself to be ahead of them in a race and took the steps necessary to be able to do that. Soon enough, my name was known around the community-- not out of fear or hatred, but as something to inspire others. People who may not have had the same advantages that other people had were telling me that I inspired them to go after what they want. That is important to me because I didn't have everything handed to me either. I constantly have to struggle in the dark to reach the light. It resonates with me. This is to show you that even though you may not have started with the advantages that others have, you could make them yourself even if it takes time. Six years for me, that's a lot of patience. Even though I did have supporters, I also had doubters. Some people told me that I was too short to make it. Other athletes laughed at me when they met me in person before a race -- until the only thing they saw was my back towards them. I've been underrated and underestimated but the only effect that has had on me is to make me stronger than I have ever been before.

In your business at times, you may feel that you are incompetent for the work laid out in front of you. Take it step by step -- day by day. Play it smart and you will eventually make it.

Right before the day I graduated from high school, I competed in the State Championships.

## Help Others

Quite recently, I've been receiving more and more appreciation from people who tell me how much I've inspired them to become better. Sometimes, they tell me that I inspired them and gave them the final push to go after their dreams. It's not too often, but when it does happen, it gives me the warmest feeling. I feel that when I help others even indirectly, it gives me meaning to do what I do. Sometimes, our most fulfilling achievements are when we help others achieve theirs. This is different from the way than what most of society thinks. Too many people think that there is a limited quantity of success available for them. They also think that if someone offers them help, they feel that they are seen as less for even being offered help. They feel as if they were seen that they were incompetent to do something so they need a little extra push. Their ego gets in the way of their success. They think that it's either "me or them" who will achieve success. If somebody else wins, that's one less opportunity for me right? This kind of thinking breeds selfishness. In a world where people are becoming increasingly more and more about themselves, thinking about the welfare of others can bring us total freedom. Another person being successful does not mean you can't be successful. In fact, the opposite is true. If you help someone become successful -- if you are with them every step of the way and support them, their success is your success. Realize that with the help others, you can go even further. Realize that if you help others, they can go even further. I have hope that we were all born with an innate need to help others. I want to leave this world better than the way I found it. I want to contribute as much as I can to help others in need. Let's bring each other up.

**Aspire Higher**

*What if a child dreamed of becoming something other than what society had intended? What if a child aspired to something greater? -Jor El*

My goal with writing this book was to teach you how to innovate and inspire you to have a mindset of higher thinking. Having higher thinking does not mean to think you are higher than others, rather, to think differently. Be confident enough that you are different from others but humble enough to know that you are not better than them. Knowing that you are different from others will keep you from comparing yourself with them. It is like comparing an apple with a chair. They are different and you can't really make a comparison between the two without stretching it. Everyone has their own path in life even though it may look similar so don't compare your footsteps with someone else's. The only time you should look to see what others are doing is to learn from them. Gain knowledge from them. To aspire higher is to break through the barriers that are placed in front of you. It is to break free from the pressure of others and to think for yourself. There are people who are going to tell you that you can't do something. Don't listen to them. In my experience, people have always told me that they are too afraid to go after their own dreams because they are afraid of what others will think. They are afraid of standing out and doing something out of the ordinary. They would rather be safe and content with just "okay" than to pursue their dreams and become "great" even if it means failing and going through struggles. It's not to say that they are worse than people going after their dreams. They have the potential to also go after their dreams and that alone is very powerful. I try to unlock the potential in others so they can tap into it. I want others to become the best version of themselves so they live their life without having regrets. I'm chasing my dreams. I hope you do too.

# I Must Go, My People Need Me

As I wrap this book up, I hope you've enjoyed reading and learning about different strategies you can use for your business today. I wanted to incorporate practical information that would make it easy for you to understand and use. Rest assured that with this information you've been learning you will create a better business through not just increasing your revenue and gaining customers but also through building the culture of your business influenced by the inspiration I wished to pass on to you.

If you enjoyed this book, I just ask of you to leave a quick three sentence review on Amazon. Having positive reviews helps me spread this information to even more people so they can learn what you've learned as well. I read every single review and if possible, I reach out to as much people as I can to let them know that their review went a long way for me and I appreciate it.

If you'd like to check me out on social media/online, here is how you can reach me:

- Personal Instagram: @mnchen_

- My brand's Instagram: @aspirehigher_

- Website: michaelchen.biz

During the time this was written, I was working on establishing a subscription box business called Sprightly. It blends nutritional fuel and inspiration in a monthly box.

- Facebook: facebook.com/sprightlybox

- Instagram: @sprightlybox

- Twitter: @sprightlybox

I'm the Marketing Director of Peerbuds, an online personal tutor startup where you can teach or learn anything you want:

- Peerbuds.com

If you'd like to reach me personally to leave your opinion or just want to talk:

- Email: michaelnchen96@gmail.com

I'd like to thank everyone who has been with me on this journey. It has definitely been a roller coaster but you all make it possible to enjoy the ride.

Now, go out and use The Art of Marketing to paint your picture.

Kindest Regards,

Michael Chen